STECK-VAUGHN
PORTRAIT OF AMERICA

Alaska

Steck-Vaughn Company

Executive Editor	Diane Sharpe
Senior Editor	Martin S. Saiewitz
Design Manager	Pamela Heaney
Photo Editor	Margie Foster

Proof Positive/Farrowlyne Associates, Inc.
Program Editorial, Revision Development, Design, and Production

Reviewer: Joan M. Antonson, State Historian, Alaska Office of History and Archaeology

Published by Raintree Steck-Vaughn Publishers, an imprint of Steck-Vaughn Company.

A Turner Educational Services, Inc. book. Based on the Portrait of America television series by R. E. (Ted) Turner.

Cover Photo: Mark Kelley/Alaska Stock Images

Library of Congress Cataloging-in-Publication Data

Thompson, Kathleen.
    Alaska / Kathleen Thompson.
       p. cm. — (Portrait of America)
    "Based on the Portrait of America television series" — T.p. verso.
    "A Turner book."
    Includes index.
    ISBN 0-8114-7322-8 (library binding). ISBN 0-8114-7427-5 (softcover).
       1. Alaska—Juvenile literature. [1. Alaska.] I. Portrait of America (Television program) II. Title.
III. Series: Thompson, Kathleen. Portrait of America.
F904.3.T46 1996
979.8—dc20   95-38325
                                 CIP
                                 AC

Acknowledgments
The publishers wish to thank the following for permission to reproduce photographs:
P. 7 © John Hyde/Alaska Stock Images; p. 8 © Chlaus Lotscher/Alaska Stock Images; pp. 10, 11, 12 (top) Alaska State Library; p. 12 (bottom) Alaska Division of Tourism; p. 13 USDA Forest Service; p. 14 Alaska State Library; p. 15 Alaska Division of Tourism; p. 16 Special Collections, Suzzallo Library, University of Washington; p. 17 (top) Alaska Railroad Collection, (bottom) Alaska State Library; p. 18 Alaska State Library; p. 19 AP/Wide World; p. 20 Kotzebue Middle/High School; p. 21 Alaska Division of Tourism; p. 22 (left) Alaska Division of Tourism, (right) Russ Weston; p. 23 Courtesy Paul Ongtooguk; p. 24 H. Hammond; p. 25 UPI/Bettmann; p. 26 © Rex Melton/Alaska Division of Tourism; p. 27 H. Hammond; p. 28 Alaska Fish & Wildlife; p. 30 (top) ARCO Alaska, (bottom) © Johnny Johnson/Alaska Stock Images; p. 31 Fairbanks Convention & Visitors Bureau/Suzanne Stolpe; p. 32 Courtesy Steve D. Culver; p. 33 Alaska Railroad Collection; p. 35 # I. A. 131 Sheldon Jackson Museum, Sitka, Alaska. Photograph by Stephen E. Hildon; p. 36 (both) Alaska State Library; p. 37 (top, bottom) Sitka National Historic Park, National Park Service, (right) # I. A. 402 Sheldon Jackson Museum, Sitka, Alaska. Photograph by Ernest Manewal; p. 38 (top) # I. A. 290 Sheldon Jackson Museum, Sitka, Alaska. Photograph by Ernest Manewal, (bottom left) # I. A. 109 Sheldon Jackson Museum, Sitka, Alaska. Photograph by Ernest Manewal, (bottom right) Alaska Division of Tourism; p. 39 (top, bottom left) Sitka National Historic Park, National Park Service, (bottom right) Provided by the Alaska Department of Commerce and Economic Development; pp. 40, 41 Alaska Division of Tourism; p. 42 © Johnny Johnson/Alaska Stock Images; p. 44 Alaska Division of Tourism; p. 46 One Mile Up; p. 47 (top left, top right) Alaska Division of Tourism, (bottom) One Mile Up.

STECK-VAUGHN
PORTRAIT OF AMERICA

Alaska

Kathleen Thompson

A Turner Book

RSVP

RAINTREE
STECK-VAUGHN
PUBLISHERS
The Steck-Vaughn Company

Austin, Texas

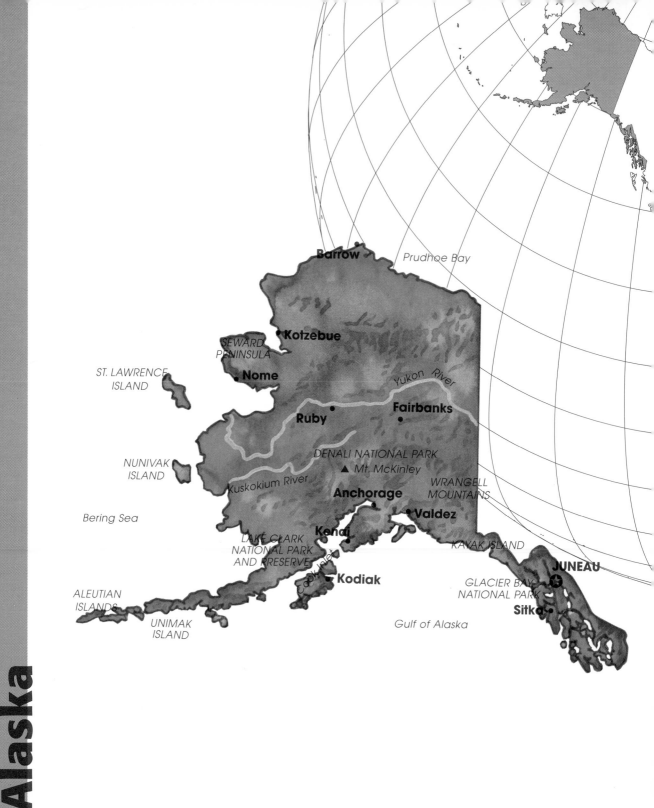

Alaska

Barrow
Prudhoe Bay
Kotzebue
SEWARD
PENINSULA
ST. LAWRENCE
ISLAND
Nome
Yukon   River
Ruby
Fairbanks
NUNIVAK
ISLAND
DENALI NATIONAL PARK
▲ Mt. McKinley
WRANGELL
MOUNTAINS
Kuskokium River
Anchorage
Bering Sea
Valdez
Kenai
KAYAK ISLAND
LAKE CLARK
NATIONAL PARK
AND PRESERVE
Cook Inlet
JUNEAU
ALEUTIAN
ISLANDS
Kodiak
GLACIER BAY
NATIONAL PARK
UNIMAK
ISLAND
Gulf of Alaska
Sitka

Contents

Introduction

What thoughts come to mind with the phrases wide-open spaces, towering mountains, and local people hunting and fishing for their food? They sound like a description of the Old West. But they also fit Alaska. In the words of the state motto, it's "North to the Future" for today's new pioneers. They are attracted by Alaska's promises of unspoiled wilderness, rich mineral resources, and a challenging natural environment. Alaska is a land of extremes. It is far and away the largest state in the nation. It is also the most northern—and the iciest. Although it was probably the first place on the continent touched by human beings, Alaska remains one of the least populated. Yet it is America's last—and most glorious—frontier.

Alaska is a state with beautiful natural scenery and abundant wildlife.

Alaska

salmon, northern lights

Land of the Last Frontier

The land now known as Alaska is the place where North America was discovered. Archaeologists believe that ancient peoples migrated from present-day Siberia to Alaska at least 15,000 years ago. At that time these two areas were connected by land. That was during the last Ice Age. Eventually, as the ice melted, the sea level rose until the land area was underwater. Now a body of water called the Bering Strait divides the area between Siberia and Alaska.

The Tlingit (pronounced *Klink-it*) lived in villages along the southeastern seacoast. They were hunters and fishers. During the winter the Tlingit devoted themselves to culture and recreation. They were outstanding carvers, woodworkers, and weavers.

The Athabascans of the interior and Cook Inlet areas were nomads who followed migrating herds of caribou. They were also hunters and fishers, trading furs and salmon with the Inuit and other Native American groups.

These dancers are Gwitch'in Athabascans from Arctic Village, located in northeast Alaska near the Brooks Range and the Arctic National Wildlife Refuge.

This drawing depicts an Aleut man who lived in the Aleutian Islands in the 1800s. These islands were the first part of this state visited by Europeans.

The Inuit lived in the north, west, and Prince William Sound areas. They hunted the oceans for whales, walrus, and seals; on land they hunted bears and caribou. In the summer, when the tundra bloomed, they gathered berries.

The Aleuts settled on the string of islands that extend southwest from the mainland to far out in the Pacific Ocean. These islands are now called the Aleutian Islands. The Aleuts depended mainly on the oceans for survival. In their skin-covered boats called *baidarkas*, they sailed hundreds of miles to hunt, trade, visit, and even raid enemy villages. The word *Alaska* comes from the Aleut word *Alyeska*, which means "Great Land."

Until the 1700s, Europeans knew very little about northeast Asia and the northwestern part of North America. Peter I, the czar of Russia, wanted to know if his country was attached to North America. In 1725 he hired a Danish sea captain, Vitus Bering, to find out.

Bering had to travel six thousand miles across Russia and Asia to reach the Pacific Ocean. He then built a ship and sailed farther north. In 1728 he passed through the Bering Strait. During this trip Bering visited and named St. Lawrence Island, a part of modern Alaska in the Bering Sea.

In 1741 Bering undertook a second expedition to Alaska. This time Aleksei Chirikov, a Russian explorer, accompanied him. During the trip they lost their way and each other's ships in a storm. Bering and Chirikov then explored separately. Bering explored near the mouth of the Copper River, south of Prince William Sound, and landed on Kayak Island. He and thirty of his crew died during the difficult voyage, but the rest of the crew returned home the next year.

This second expedition brought back one exceptional thing—sea otter furs. Few Russians had ever seen sea otter furs before. The furs were sold to China. The desire for furs spread quickly. The battle for the wealth of Alaska's natural resources was on. Soon the Aleutian Islands were overrun by Russian fur traders trying to make a quick fortune. They killed or enslaved the Aleuts, who were easy to conquer because they were isolated on different islands.

The Russians' interest in the North Pacific soon got the attention of other countries. Great Britain and Spain made claims to the region. Spain had long claimed all of the Pacific Coast from Mexico to the Arctic Circle. In 1778 they included the Alaskan coast in their claim.

British Captain James Cook arrived in Alaska that same year. However, he was looking for a Northwest Passage—a northern water route from the Atlantic Ocean to the Pacific Ocean. After sailing as far north as the Bering Strait without finding the passage, Cook left to spend the winter in Hawaii. He was killed there, but his crew returned to Alaska in 1779. They collected fur pelts that they sold later in China.

Vitus Bering led two major expeditions that mapped the coasts of Siberia, in Russia, and present-day Alaska.

11

Gregory Shelikov founded Alaska's first trading post on Kodiak Island.

Several years later the Russians made their presence in Alaska more formal. In 1784 Gregory Shelikov founded the first permanent European settlement in Alaska on Kodiak Island. Meanwhile, Spain was ready to assert its claim. In 1787 Spanish explorers arrived to select a good place for a settlement. After choosing a site near Nootka, the Spanish left. When they came back the next year, they found the British had settled on their site. The Spanish seized the British ships, and the two countries almost went to war. By 1792 Spain had given up its claim.

The British continued exploring the northwestern coast. Captain George Vancouver charted many of the islands and inlets; his influence shows in British names along the southeastern coastline.

Russian settlers built this cathedral at Sitka.

This Russian Orthodox church at Kenai marks the second-oldest Russian settlement in America.

In 1799 the Russians reinforced their claim on Alaska. Czar Paul I chartered the Russian-American Company, granting it complete trading rights. The Russian-American Company took control of the fur trade and governed the region. In 1808 the company's headquarters moved from Kodiak to New Archangel (later renamed Sitka), on Kodiak Island.

Aleksandr Baranov was governor of the area from 1800 to 1818. Under Baranov the company substantially increased its fur harvest and established several settlements. A strict manager, he treated the native people severely. His treatment led to a Tlingit uprising in 1802. Russians were massacred and Sitka was destroyed. The town was rebuilt two years later as the capital of Russian America.

During the early 1800s, the United States also became involved in trading furs. The Russian, British, and American fur traders were in fierce competition. Aleksandr Baranov retired in 1818. After about 1820, the Russian-American Company was managed by Russian naval officers. During this time the Russians explored the region and assessed its resources. They built schools and iron foundries. They carried out smallpox inoculations. They also developed trading routes, coal mining, farming, and sheep raising.

In 1824 Russia signed a treaty with the United States allowing Americans to trade in Alaska. The treaty also set the southeastern boundary. The next year Russia signed a trade agreement with Great Britain and established the eastern boundary. The treaties solved political problems but decreased the company's profits—and almost wiped out the sea otter population. With less profits from the fur trade, the Russians became less interested in Alaska. In addition, Russia was involved in a very costly war from 1853 to 1856. The Russians feared losing Alaska to the British, with whom they had been fighting. For these reasons, the Russian government offered to sell Alaska to the United States.

Negotiations between Russia and the United States began in the 1850s but were delayed by the Civil War. Finally, in 1867, Russia made a formal proposal that the United States accepted. The United States paid Russia $7,200,000—about two cents per acre—for Alaska. Secretary of State William Seward was the most outspoken in favor of the purchase.

During the early years of United States control, some people called the purchase "Seward's Folly." These people felt that having Alaska was useless, since a lot of good farmland in the western United States was not even settled. Yet Americans moved quickly to take control of the Russian-American Company posts, to trade along the Yukon River, and to exploit the profitable fur trade.

Civil government was established in 1884 when Congress passed the Organic Act. This act applied Oregon's laws to Alaska. During this time, a court system and a school system were established.

Fishing grew in importance, and in 1878 the first salmon canneries were opened. During the late nineteenth century, the existence of sea otters, fur seals, walrus, salmon, and whales in the area was threatened. The native people's lives depended on these animals. To increase the food supply, the federal government in 1891 brought reindeer from Siberia for the native peoples to herd. Sheldon Jackson, a missionary and educator who established schools in Alaska, led this program.

Alaskan crabs are usually caught with pots or traps. Fish traps are designed so that fish, shrimp, or crab can swim inside for shelter but can't get back out. This man is shown with his day's catch of crabs.

In 1896 large deposits of gold were discovered in the Klondike. This area is in Canada's Yukon Territory, just across the Alaska-Canada border. Around one hundred thousand prospectors made the difficult and complex trip through Alaska to the Yukon. Serving the prospectors' needs on the way caused tremendous growth in Alaska. One result was a number of new towns, such as Skagway and Valdez.

The Canadian gold rush was barely over when there was another gold strike on the Seward Peninsula in northwest Alaska at the turn of the century. By mid-1900 about ten thousand people crowded into Nome. There was no effective government or police force to maintain order. That made it necessary to pass a code of criminal and civil laws.

Other important gold discoveries were made around Fairbanks in 1902 and in the Yellow and Iditarod river valleys in 1906. Ruby, along the Yukon River, had a run of gold from 1907 to 1910. Copper ore was mined in the Copper River basin near McCarthy from 1911 to 1938.

Juneau was made the official capital of Alaska in 1900. In 1906 Alaskans elected their first representative to Congress. Because Alaska was not a state, however, Delegate Frank H. Waskey could not vote on issues. In 1912 Congress passed another Organic Act. This act made Alaska a United States territory and set up a territorial legislature.

This is how Skagway's main business street looked in October 1897, during the Klondike gold rush.

A team of horses is used to haul the locomotive "Dinky" to Riley Creek during the building of the Alaska Railroad.

After the gold rush period, Alaska's population dropped. The economy relied on fishing, mining, and fur trading. With government aid, experimental farms were established in the valleys near Fairbanks in 1917. The Alaska Railroad was completed in 1923. It linked Seward and Anchorage on the coast with Fairbanks in the interior. During the 1920s and the 1930s, the Alaskan economy grew slowly. Small airplanes linked remote areas with the territory's larger towns. In the 1930s Alaskans worked to develop agriculture.

On an Alaskan farm in the early 1900s, three girls harvest cauliflower.

In 1941 Fort Mears was constructed at Dutch Harbor in the Aleutian Islands. One year later, during World War II, the Japanese invaded Alaska and bombed Dutch Harbor.

World War II brought major changes to Alaska. In 1942 the Japanese bombed Dutch Harbor and occupied Attu and Kiska islands in the Aleutians. Aware of Alaska's strategic location near Asia, the United States built military bases and a supply road, the Alaska Highway. The United States recaptured Attu and Kiska in 1943. After the war the military buildup continued in Alaska. The United States enlarged military bases, set up radar systems, and built roads across the territory. Alaska's economic development increased as a result.

During the 1950s Alaska expanded and modernized its fishing, canning, and timber-processing industries. In 1957 commercial oil fields in the Kenai Peninsula-Cook Inlet region were discovered. This discovery helped to establish the petroleum industry in Alaska.

The increase in population and the growing economy made a strong case for statehood. On January 3, 1959, Alaska became the forty-ninth state. In 1963 and 1964, Alaska opened parts of the Marine Highway system, linking towns along the coast. Also in 1964 south-central Alaska was hit by a severe earthquake, measuring 8.4 on the Richter scale. Parts of Anchorage sank thirty feet in only a few seconds. A huge tidal wave caused by the quake destroyed coastal areas. In 1971 the Alaska Native Claims Settlement Act gave $962.5 million and 44 million acres to Alaska's native peoples.

The Alaskan pipeline was completed in 1977.

A new era in Alaska began in 1968 with the discovery of great petroleum and natural-gas deposits around Prudhoe Bay. It was decided to send the oil by pipeline to the port of Valdez, where it could be transferred to tanker ships. Many people objected to the project. The main reason was that the pipeline might damage the ecological balance of Alaska's interior. Congress approved the plan, however, and the Alaskan pipeline was completed in 1977 at a cost of $10 billion.

In March 1989 the Exxon *Valdez*, an oil tanker, hit a reef in Prince William Sound, spilling more than 11 million gallons of crude oil. The accident damaged several hundred miles of coastline and killed much wildlife. The cleanup cost more than $2 billion.

Land protection continued through the 1970s and the 1980s. In 1980 Congress passed the Alaska National Interest Lands Conservation Act, restricting future development on more than one hundred million acres. This act also designated about 160 million acres of land as national monuments and reserves.

Alaska is still rich in natural resources. Not only are its oil and natural gas deposits valuable but so is its unspoiled land. In the past some of the resources have been carelessly exploited. Alaska recognizes that the challenge lies in protecting these resources, while also moving steadily into the twenty-first century.

Tradition and the Inuit Way

Paul Ongtooguk, an Inupiat Inuit, is a teacher who's tired of the same old story. He wants a different story for Alaska. "The history of America is that Native Americans lose their land," he said. Mr. Ongtooguk feels that Native Americans' self-determination and culture are always under attack. "That's a sad history."

In some ways Alaska is already different. The Inuit still have their villages, although the villages have changed. They still have their land and the sea. They've had to fight very hard for what they have.

Paul Ongtooguk teaches traditional culture in native studies. He emphasizes the importance of the settlement between the native peoples and the government. As he says, "Even if you're not hunting on it (and most Alaskan natives are) and even if you don't derive a good part of your food off of that land (which most Alaskan natives are doing), it's important to know that it's still there, and that it's still ours."

The village of Kotzebue had to learn that lesson the hard way. The second-largest Inuit town, Kotzebue found itself facing some very serious problems, including family abuse and alcohol and drug abuse. Something had gone wrong.

Classes at Kotzebue teach traditional skills.

Inuits traditionally travel by dogsled in the winter.

John Schaeffer, the mayor of Kotzebue, set out to find out what was wrong and how to fix it. He talked to experts, such as psychiatrists and psychologists, but they couldn't find the answers that the mayor needed.

That's when the mayor of Kotzebue decided to turn to another kind of wisdom. He went back to the culture of his people by talking to the elders, as had been done in times past.

They told Schaeffer the problem was that values of the Inuit were not being taught to the children.

Now at Kotzebue they're working on those values. They're teaching their young ones who they really are, because they can't afford ever to forget.

Mr. Ongtooguk hopes that the three-hundred-year history of conflict between Western society and native

Alaskans will somehow turn out differently. He is concerned that native Alaskans will become another downtrodden minority. Mr. Ongtooguk believes that Inuits and Western society have an opportunity now to live together in mutual respect.

Paul Ongtooguk would say that Kotzebue has learned a lesson about

An Inuit couple appears with a dog team. They are wearing parkas, traditional coats, which are shaped like oversized shirts with hoods.

John Schaeffer, former mayor of Kotzebue, turned to the town elders to find solutions for problems in Kotzebue.

Paul Ongtooguk is an Inupiat Inuit teacher who brings traditional culture into the classroom.

the importance of tradition. The role of the elders has always been to apply the wisdom of age to the group's most important problems. As the Inuit look to the future, they must face Alaska's challenge: to use the wisdom of the past to find a way into the future.

Wilderness Life

For many people, Alaska is the "Final Frontier," the last place in the United States that they can go to find untamed wilderness. Jay Hammond, governor of the state from 1974 to 1982 is one of those people. In fact, you could call Jay Hammond the ultimate Alaskan. The former governor has been a fisherman and a bush pilot. He has hosted a series of television programs called "Jay Hammond's Alaska."

Hammond lives at Lake Clark Lodge, in the Lake Clark National Park and Preserve. He can't imagine living anywhere else. "Things are etched in more vivid colors. We live in extremes.

Jay Hammond served two terms as governor.

We're the farthest north, the coldest, the smallest communities, and the biggest state." Some of Jay's best memories are from the years when he was a bush pilot. Bush pilots are essential for traveling in remote areas of

Hammond was a bush pilot for years before becoming governor.

In the backcountry, where there are no runways, a float plane can make a landing on any available body of water.

Alaska because the state is so large and many areas have no roads. It's the job of a bush pilot to fly passengers and supplies to places that could not be reached otherwise. Sometimes the pilots have to land their planes on glaciers or on lakes—no matter what the weather is like. It's a dangerous profession. But to Jay, the beauty more than makes up for the danger.

"It's spiritual, sustaining" he says. "It blows the cobwebs out of the soul, to see that sort of wilderness . . . unfold beneath you. You're living on the edge. . . . Just the fact that you've lived through the day is exhilarating."

For Jay Hammond, Alaska offers wilderness and adventure in a world that's become too tame. Alaska is the wide-open land and all the challenge in the world. And living in Alaska means being strong enough to meet that challenge. That makes all the hardship worthwhile.

Jay Hammond uses a pump to extract water from one of his plane's pontoons.

Seward's Treasure Chest

They once called Alaska "Seward's Folly." After the Civil War, Secretary of State William H. Seward saw the region as being vitally important to the United States. He negotiated the purchase of Alaska in 1867. Today, Alaska's riches—its gold, silver, copper, oil, and other mineral deposits—have made some people call Alaska "Seward's Treasure Chest." It's certainly true that mining has been an important source of wealth.

That fact became very obvious when oil was discovered at Prudhoe Bay, on Alaska's North Slope, above the Arctic Circle. The oil field at Prudhoe Bay is the biggest in North America. To make sure that everyone in Alaska benefited from its resources, Alaskans passed an amendment to their state constitution. The amendment created the Alaska Permanent Fund, a savings account made up of 25 percent of the profits from mineral development. When oil prices are high—and so is oil production—the fund pays everyone's state income taxes. It also pays a cash dividend to every citizen.

Alaska's commericial fishing industry brings in nearly $1.5 million for the state each year. Alaska's most important fishing ports are Ketchikan and Bristol Bay.

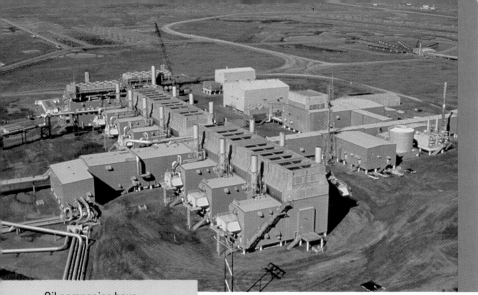

Oil companies have designed special oil rigs to prevent damage to the fragile Arctic tundra.

These caribou are grazing on the tundra in Alaska's interior.

Because oil prices have dropped, the income from the pipeline isn't as much today. Nevertheless, Alaska is still second only to Texas in oil production. Plus, Alaska has other natural resources. There are rich fields of natural gas. The Red Dog zinc mine is the largest in the Northern Hemisphere. Add to that huge deposits of lead, molybdenum—and more gold. New mining technology has increased the profit level of mining all of these hard rock ore deposits.

Alaska's natural riches aren't just found under the ground. Today's commercial fishing brings even more money into the state than minerals do. Salmon account for most of the state's fishing harvest. Every year the Alaskan fisheries bring in load after load of salmon as well as shrimp, herring, cod, pollack, halibut, and crab. In fact, Alaska harvests more fish than any other state.

Service industries play a major part in the Alaskan economy, contributing about half of the gross state product. The state and federal governments contribute about 12 percent of the total. The state's biggest employer is actually the federal government. That's because Alaska is in a strategic military location, and many military personnel are stationed on bases in Alaska.

Alaska annually attracts thousands of tourists. Many are interested in the beautiful scenery. National Park Service land totals about 51 million acres. This land provides many opportunities for outdoor recreation, such as hiking, fishing, skiing, and rock climbing—not to mention mountain climbing.

Agriculture is only a very small part of Alaska's economy. The chief farm products are milk, eggs, greenhouse plants, hay, and potatoes. The state has just a few hundred farms. The lower Matanuska River valley, near Anchorage, is the principal cropland. Today, three quarters of the farm products of the state come from this area.

Most of Alaska's livestock are reindeer. They are raised in the Tanana River valley, near Fairbanks, and in areas of the southeastern part of the state. Some sheep and cattle are also raised. Alaskans also raise horses, which are used as pack animals.

Fur trapping, on a small scale, provides a significant source of income for some people. Harvesting of moose, caribou, seals, and whales is very important to the livelihood of native Alaskans.

Glacier Bay National Monument has 16 glaciers. Glacier Bay is a good place to see whales, seals, birds, mountain goats, and brown bears.

Riding Alaskan Rails

The Alaska Railroad was completed in 1923. It provides freight and passenger services from Seward and Whittier to Anchorage along the coast, and on to Fairbanks in the interior of the state. The route runs through four hundred miles of wilderness forest. Sometimes the train has to stop for moose or caribou that have wandered onto the tracks. It sometimes has to stop for Alaskans who want to get on the train between stations.

Many people don't go to a train station to get on the Alaska Railroad. There just aren't very many train stations along the line. There is too much land and too few people in the state. To get on the Alaska Railroad, you only have to flag down the train. Conductor Steve Culver explains the process. "You just step up next to the tracks and wave back and forth, and the engineer'll give you a couple of toots when he sees you." People wanting to ride don't have to look at a schedule. "We pull right up like a taxicab and spot the train right alongside them. They load everything in the baggage car, jump on the train, and away we go."

The atmosphere is friendly on the Alaska Railroad. Many of the people who ride it live in the back country. The train ride gives them one of their few chances to chat with their

Conductor Steve Culver watches passengers board the Alaska Railroad at Denali National Park.

The Alaska Railroad passes close by Riley Creek.

neighbors, since their neighbors may live many miles down the tracks.

The Alaska Railroad services towns, villages, and groups of cabins too small even to be called villages. In the wilderness areas, you don't find any highways. In some cases, there's not even a real road to the train track.

Conductor Culver explains how to run a railroad without stations. "They tell me when they get on where they want to go. They'll say, 'I'm going to 238.4'. . . I know 238.4 is a bridge, there's a trail off the side of the bridge and there's several cabins as far as 12 miles back.''

The Alaska Railroad certainly is one of a kind. That's because it provides the extra service of stopping for waving passengers. One almost believes that, if it could, it would pull up to people's doorsteps to offer them a ride.

Northern Arts

The best-known art of Alaska is the art of native Alaskans. Native cultures, which are thousands of years old, still thrive across the state. Although many native Alaskans have moved away from their traditional areas, they have taken their culture with them. The techniques of creating their art are handed down from one generation to the next.

Before Russian settlement, the Tlingit culture flourished in southeast Alaska, along the coast of the Pacific Ocean. Tlingit society was divided into two groups, Raven and Wolf or Eagle. Each group was further divided into clans. Each clan was represented by particular animals, such as a bear or a whale. Artists of a particular clan used these representative symbols throughout their art.

One place that clan animals often appear is in the Tlingit's beautifully carved totem poles. Other figures carved on the poles may relate a story or celebrate an important event. For example, after the United States purchased Alaska, Secretary of State Seward went to

Katlean, a Tlingit war leader, wore this helmet in a battle with Russians in 1804. The helmet represents the Raven Clan.

above. These men are dressed in traditional Tlingit clothing.

right. This photo shows a traditional Tlingit clan house.

visit. The Tlingit held a potlatch in his honor. A *potlatch* is a dinner celebration during which gifts are exchanged. Seward didn't realize that the guest also should give a gift to the hosts. The Tlingits, a proud people, were insulted. So when they carved a totem pole expressing the event, they made Seward's likeness very unflattering.

The art of wood carving was not used on totem poles only. Each traditional Tlingit clan had at least one important lodge. The posts of this main house were elaborately carved and painted. Inside, on the back wall, carved cedar planks exhibited the clans

A Tlingit carver works on a totem pole.

symbols. The lodge's storage chests were also beautifully carved and sometimes painted.

The art of the Tlingits extended beyond handmade objects. A traditional Tlingit name often employed creative word play, much like a poem does. For example, a baby girl might be given the name "Sunshine Glinting." If her father is from the whale clan, part of her name would reflect that fact. Her full name, then, would form a creative line such as "Sunshine Glinting on the Dorsal Fin of the Whale as It Rises."

This ornamental Tlingit basket is made of finely split spruce root. The basket was woven before 1888.

Some totem poles include humorous figures.

Other native Alaskan groups add their own special perspective to the culture of the state. The Athabascan have mastered the art of fine beadwork. The Aleuts are known especially for their finely carved fishing implements made of bone or ivory. They are excellent basket weavers, too.

The Inuit of northern Alaska are also well-known for their carvings. They specialize in symbolic representations of Inuit life and of the animals of the far north. A favorite medium for these carvings is soapstone, which is found near the seashore. Inuit artists also carve in ivory, which is obtained from walrus tusks. The sculptors carve familiar figures, often of the animals they hunt.

Four salmon grace the front of this Tlingit shirt. The floral border at the bottom of the shirt is typical of Tlingit beadwork.

above. This Tlingit charm is carved out of ivory. It depicts a sea monster.

right. This woman, a native of Alaska, is shown weaving a basket.

The rich traditional culture of the Alaskan peoples still lives today. And it affects all modern artists, no matter what their cultural heritage. To make sure Alaskan artists get the recognition they deserve when their art is sold, Alaska has adopted a "Silver Hand" logo. This symbol identifies the work as authentic Alaskan Native handicraft.

above. These totem poles are displayed at Sitka National Park.

below. In 1993 the Alaska Legislature adopted the Silver Hand logo, which certifies that a work of art was produced by a native Alaskan.

This totem pole stands in Ketchikan in southeast Alaska.

AUTHENTIC NATIVE HANDICRAFT FROM ALASKA

The Challenge of the Iditarod

Every year, one of the most famous and most difficult races in the world takes place in Alaska. It is not an auto race, a horse race, or a foot race. It is the Iditarod Trail Sled Dog Race. The course begins in Anchorage and ends in Nome—a distance of 1,150 miles!

The first Iditarod took place in 1973. On that day, 22 sled teams managed to reach the finish line. The winning team needed more than twenty days to complete the race. Today, contestants usually finish the race in 10 to 13 days. A sled dog racer is called a *musher*. Mushers come from many different countries to partake in this grueling race. Men and women often compete together.

Rick Swenson holds the record for number of wins. He has won the race five times. Susan Butcher has won four times. Martin Buser, who won twice, is the only other person to win more than once.

Preparation is critical. Mushers are required to ship their food ahead to

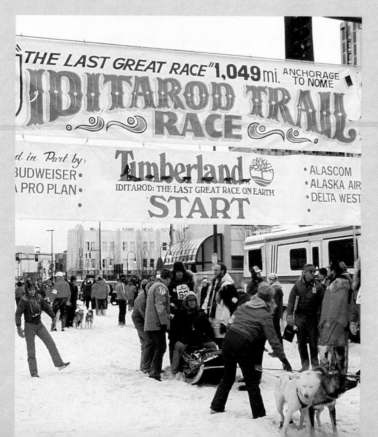

The Iditarod starts every year in downtown Anchorage in early March. On the way to Nome, the mushers stop in small towns where local residents put them up overnight and help care for the dogs.

twenty checkpoints along the way. During the race they will stop at these places to eat while they rest their teams.

Sled teams are on the move for most of each day and night. The Iditarod trail crosses two mountain ranges, runs along the Yukon River for 150 miles, and crosses frozen waterways. Snowstorms are common, and temperatures can sink to 40 or 50 degrees Fahrenheit below zero. Participants must guard against frostbite. Some mushers wear so many layers of clothes that sometimes it is difficult to steer the sled.

Each sled is pulled by as many as 15 dogs. Pulling a sled through deep snow and freezing cold is hard work. The dogs are checked carefully throughout the race for injury. Each dog's paws must be rubbed with ointment to prevent infection. That's sixty paws to look after! The dogs are also given a snack every hour. At this time their harnesses are removed and each dog is given a rubdown. The team is also given three hot meals a day.

The mushers have to drive their teams through some very rough country. One such place is Rainy Pass, a gorge full of snow-covered boulders.

The lead dog of a team has to be smart enough to understand the musher's directions, such as haw, *which means left, and* gee, *which means right. Mushers never tell their dogs to mush. Instead, they say, "hike!" or "let's go!"*

A sled that hits one of these boulders can tip over or even break, leaving a team stranded. Another dangerous place is known to racers as "The Burn." It is an area full of burned-down tree stumps. The stumps are so close together in places that the sleds can become jammed between them. Some racers have had to use saws to cut their sleds free.

Crossing the finish line is an emotional moment for many racers. Some burst into tears. They are proud of themselves and their dogs. They have worked together to meet the challenge. And in spite of the difficulty, or maybe because of it, many racers promise they will do it again.

Expanding—
and Protecting—
the Frontier

To consider Alaska's future, you have to remember just how big this state is—one fifth the size of the rest of the United States. Then you have to look at Alaska's diversity. It has mountains, lowlands, temperate southern islands, and the frigid Arctic north. Alaska also has ocean fields of fish and other sea life. All of this has been the basis for Alaska's growth.

The natural resources will play a major role in Alaska's future, too. Oil, gas, fish, forests, minerals—people want and need these resources all over the world. Alaska is uniquely positioned to serve those needs. Its neighbors are Canada and Russia, and parts of Alaska stretch far out toward Asian nations. International trade is already a major part of Alaska's economy. That trend will continue.

But Alaskans know from experience how hard it is to protect its natural richness. The state has experienced unchallenged and unrestrained development. The result? Fur hunters nearly wiped out the sea otters. The whaling fleet pushed the whales and the walrus to

Many tourists visit Alaska on cruise ships like this one, which is gliding through Gastineau Channel, near Juneau.

the edge of extinction. More recently, the fragile nature of Alaskan wildlife became all too clear in the oil-coated bodies of birds and mammals killed in the Exxon *Valdez* disaster.

Alaska is a frontier facing a challenge. Alaskans will have to balance the value of that frontier with the value of the natural resources. All states face this problem. But it is more serious in Alaska because Alaska's wilderness is important to its diverse peoples—and to the people of the United States.

Alaska has much of its development ahead. It stands to benefit from all the mistakes the other states have made. Alaska still has its wilderness, its wildlife, and some of its native culture intact. With all its riches, Alaska can be a place where progress does not have to go wrong.

Anchorage is Alaska's largest city and the center of its economy. Many of the future decisions regarding the state's natural resources will come from business leaders in this city.

Important Historical Events

1728 Vitus Bering explores the Bering Strait and lands on St. Lawrence Island.

1741 Bering sets out on a second expedition with Russian explorer Aleksei Chirikov. Bering's crew lands on Kayak Island.

1778 British Captain James Cook explores the area while looking for a Northwest Passage.

1784 Gregory Shelikov establishes the first European settlement in Alaska, on Kodiak Island.

1792 Spain yields all claims in the North Pacific to the British.

1792 to 1794 Captain George Vancouver makes a detailed exploration of the Alaskan coast.

1799 Russia charters the Russian-American Company to control fur trade. Aleksandr Baranov is made manager.

1802 Tlingit Native Americans destroy Fort St. Michael at Sitka.

1818 Russian naval officers take charge of the Russian-American Company.

1824 to 1825 Russians sign treaties with the United States and Great Britain, setting boundaries and allowing trading rights.

1861 The charter expires for the Russian-American Company.

1867 The United States buys Alaska from Russia.

1878 The first canneries open in Alaska.

1884 Congress passes the first Organic Act, which gives Alaska a civil government.

1896 Gold is discovered in the Canadian Klondike.

1897 Gold prospectors pour through Skagway into the Yukon Territory.

1898 Gold is discovered at Nome; copper is discovered in the Wrangell Mountains.

1902 Gold is discovered near Fairbanks.

1903 A border dispute between Canada and the United States is resolved.

1906 Frank H. Waskey is elected the first Alaskan delegate to Congress.

1912 Congress passes the second Organic Act, giving Alaska a territorial legislature.

1923 The Alaska Railroad is completed, linking Seward, Anchorage, and Fairbanks.

1942 The Japanese occupy the Aleutian Islands of Attu and Kiska. The Alaska Highway is completed.

1959 Alaska becomes the forty-ninth state.

1964 The strongest recorded earthquake in North America damages much of south-central Alaska.

1968 Oil is discovered at Prudhoe Bay. It is believed to be the largest oil field in North America.

1971 The United States Congress passes the Alaska Native Claims Settlement Act.

1977 The Alaskan pipeline is completed.

1978 President Jimmy Carter sets aside over fifty million acres in Alaska as parks and public resources.

1989 The Exxon *Valdez* oil tanker hits a reef in Prince William Sound, spilling more than 11 million gallons of crude oil and causing billions of dollars of damages.

1993 Scientists report that after employing 10,000 people and spending $2.5 million toward the cleanup of the Exxon *Valdez*, deposits of tar remain on the beaches.

The blue field is for the sky and the forget-me-not, the state flower. The North Star represents the future of Alaska, the most northerly of the United States. The dipper symbolizes the strength of the Great Bear.

Alaska Almanac

Nickname. The Last Frontier

Capital. Juneau

State Bird. Willow ptarmigan

State Flower. Forget-me-not

State Tree. Sitka spruce

State Motto. North to the Future

State Song. "Alaska's Flag"

State Abbreviations. Ala. (traditional); AK (postal).

Statehood. January 3, 1959, the 49th state

Government. Congress: U.S. senators, 2; U.S. representatives, 1. State Legislature: senators, 20; representatives, 40. State Divisions: 15 organized boroughs

Area. 589,878 sq mi (1,522,596 sq km), 1st in size among the states

Greatest Distances. north/south, 1,350 mi (2,150 km); east/west, 2,350 mi (3,800 km). Shoreline: 6,640 mi (10,686 km)

Population. 1990 Census: 551,947 (37% increase over 1980), 48th among the states. Density: 9.4 persons per sq mi (0.36 persons per sq km). Distribution: 67% urban, 33% rural. 1980 Census: 400,481

Economy. *Agriculture:* barley, hay, oats, potatoes, milk, eggs, beef cattle, greenhouse and nursery products. *Fishing:* salmon, shrimp, crab, halibut. *Manufacturing:* fish products, lumber and wood products, furs, stone and clay products, paper products. *Mining:* oil, natural gas, gold, sand and gravel

State Bird: Willow ptarmigan

State Flower: Forget-me-not

Annual Events

★ Russian Christmas and Starring in Kodiak (January)

★ Fur Rendezvous in Anchorage (February)

★ Iditarod Trail Sled Dog Race from Anchorage to Nome (March)

★ Alaska Folk Festival in Juneau (April)

★ Glacier Dash in Girdwood (June)

★ Kenai Peninsula State Fair in Ninilchik (August)

★ Blueberry Festival in Seldovia (September)

State Seal

Places to Visit

★ Alyeska Ski Resort, near Anchorage

★ Delta Junction, at northern end of Alaska Highway

★ Denali National Park and Preserve

★ Glacier Bay National Park

★ Kenai Fjords National Park on Kenai Peninsula

★ Kennecott Copper Mine in Wrangell

★ Kodiak National Wildlife Refuge on Kodiak Island

★ Russian Bishop's House in Sitka

★ Saint Nicholas Russian Church in Eklutna, north of Anchorage

★ Totem Heritage Center in Ketchikan

Index